Death of a Water District

Death of a Water District

*How a badly implemented
rate increase pushed one water district
to the edge of collapse*

By Leo D. Havener
and Richard A. Wilson

Published by Sentium Publishing

Copyright © 2015 Leo D. Havener and Richard A. Wilson

All rights reserved. No part of this book may be used or reproduced in any manner whatsoever without written permission of the Publisher. Printed in the United States of America. For information contact
Sentium Inc.
5170 Golden Foothill Parkway, Suite 138
El Dorado Hills, California 95762 USA
www.deathofawaterdistrict.com

Book design by Erica K. Wilson

First Edition

1 3 5 7 8 6 4 2

Foreward

By Kathleen J. Tiegs

Can you imagine placing your vote of confidence in a local elected body, only to learn that its leadership and policy-making were disingenuous? Can you imagine demanding transparency and accountability from your local elected officials, only to be deceived and misinformed in the end?

Death of a Water District is a compelling account of how the lack of bold and forthright leadership at a public utility district nearly caused its collapse. The authors share how the power of a deceived community impacted a public agency, the steps that were taken to reverse the situation, and key lessons learned.

As an elected official, I truly believe that public bodies should be held to the highest standards to ensure sound fiscal management and policies to maintain accountability and transparency.

Ratepayers expect their utility district to provide essential services based on true cost of service. In addition to administrative costs, utility districts are expected to consistently adopt and collect user fees sufficient to fund water system maintenance and operation costs, maintain an operating reserve account, and cover bond covenants.

This story is a must read for local public governing boards and managers. High performing districts require bold leadership. Bold leadership takes courage.

Kathleen J. Tiegs
Rancho Cucamonga, California

Introduction

They say that history repeats itself. But, by knowing the pitfalls of the past, one can prevent problems in the future.

The goal of this book is to help your district avoid the situation faced by the Foresthill Public Utility District.

Voters passed a ballot measure that forced the district's rates back to when the district was already hemorrhaging money.

This set a precedent that sent a cold shiver down the spine of public districts everywhere. Imagine voters deciding what they believe their rates should be with no consideration for actual costs of operation. Even worse, they are the law of the land.

Measure B assured that the Foresthill PUD would eventually collapse.

Our intention is that this book gives you an understanding of the mistakes that led Foresthill to the brink of its demise. It also tells you how the situation was turned around.

Why is this important to you? Most public utilities are making many of the same mistakes right now. The frightening fact is that history is indeed being repeated. These mistakes may even be happening in your district today.

By learning the lessons from the Foresthill PUD, you can avoid unnecessary pitfalls and steer your own district to a better future.

This story is told by two industry experts who were there. Leo Havener is a water district turnaround specialist who stepped into the general manager role. Richard Wilson is the communications consultant who was brought in to sort out the public information program needed to save the district.

Like many examples in the storied history of water, this is a narrative of controversy, mismanagement, deceit, heroes, and villains.

At the very least, this account gives some very clear lessons that every manager and board member involved with a public district should know.

Leo D. Havener   *Lake Arrowhead, California*
Richard A. Wilson   *El Dorado Hills, California*

Table of Contents:

Chapter		page number
	Foreword	i
	Introduction	iii
1	Being Thrown to the Lions	1
2	A Little Water District in California's Gold Country	3
3	Buying a Dam But Forgetting to Pay for It	7
4	False Economies	9
5	Raising Rates: A Decade of Increases All at Once	13
6	Measure B Rears its Ugly Head	17
7	With a Gun to Their Heads, the Board Wakes Up	23
8	A Stranger Comes to Town	25
9	So What Was Really Going On?	27
10	Recruiting Allies and a Strategy for Survival	31
11	An Unorthodox Plan	35
12	Building Trust	39

13	The Opposition Strikes Back.............	43
14	A Bold Gamble: Creating Measure C......	47
15	A Lucky Break	51
16	The Battle of Foresthill	55
17	The Smoke Clears, Who's Won?..........	59
18	What?................................	63
19	Lesson One: Whiskey is for Drinking; Water is for Fighting Over	67
20	Lesson Two: Unreal Rates are a Ticking Time Bomb....	71
21	Lesson Three: Treat Your District Like a Car............	75
22	Lesson Four: Can Uninformed People Make Good Decisions?..................	79
23	Lesson Five: The Time to Dig the Moat is Not When the Mongol Hoard is Cresting the Hill.....	83
24	The Next Step	87
	About the Authors.....................	90
	Putting This Information to Work for You	92

Death of a Water District

1
Being Thrown to the Lions
from Leo's journal

"Why it it that they always want to kill the messenger?

The presentation was not going well. I was stepping through a set of PowerPoint slides that explained that if Measure B was still in place a month later, the water district would be forced to close. I had finished the slide that showed that the cost of operations was not being covered four years earlier. Now the losses were even greater.

'You're lying!' A man in jeans, t-shirt, and open flannel shirt interrupted. He proceeded to fire off a string of questions. Every time I tried to answer, he cut me off and continued his rant.

Not only did he not like my information, he questioned my intelligence, my motives, and my integrity. Based on one comment he was also not so fond of my mother.

Usually, when you give a presentation for the local Lions Club, they serve a predictable chicken lunch with some potatoes and carrots. As others joined the rant, I had the distinct impression that it wasn't chicken but 'Water District General Manager' that was the main course on the menu.

I looked over at the president of the club expecting he would bring some civility to the proceedings. He simply smiled at me. His gavel stayed silent."

2

A Little Water District in California's Gold Country

This story actually begins a few years earlier.

Foresthill is a small community in California's Gold Country. It's about 15 minutes off the main highway on a road that dead-ends just beyond Foresthill.

The community was founded during the boom period of the mid-1850s. The Gold Rush had brought people from all over the world to the Foothills of the Sierra Nevada Mountains. There are still people who search the local waterways looking for gold. According to conversations around town, some people still find it.

A second economic boom came from the logging industry. The pines trees in the region are tall, straight and plentiful. In 1991, however, a federal endangered species protection ruling for the Spotted Owl brought the lumber industry to a halt in the area.

Since that time, for many people in Foresthill, "environmentalist" is a four letter word.

The public water district was formed in 1950 and was named the Foresthill Public Utility District. The locals just call it "the P-U-D."

Since there was no city government, the closest things to civic management were the PUD and the local fire department.

The community had a post office, a library, one grocery store, assorted shops and restaurants, and two places where you could buy gasoline. Wells Fargo Bank closed the only bank branch. For local banking, what was left was a lonely automated teller machine.

The residents were a mixture of people. Some "worked off the hill," commuting to the Sacramento area. Others owned local businesses or were retired. Many people were unemployed. They hoped the local economy would recover.

The water district served 1,875 residential connections and 75 businesses. It covered an area of approximately 13,000 acres. Because it served a mountainous region there were 50 miles of pipeline.

Most of the water system was put in during the early 1950s using surplus steel pipe from World War II. That pipe had a projected life span of about 40 years. Most of it had been in the ground for more than 60 years.

The jewel of the district, however, was its water source: the Sugar Pine Dam and reservoir. The reservoir was surrounded by trees and held 7,000 acre feet of water. Since most of the water came from snow melt, it was cold and crystal clear.

While the water district owned the dam and the water behind it, the US Forest Service controlled the land around the dam. Local fishermen had their own secret spots for where the best fish could be found.

In many ways, Foresthill looked like an idyllic, picture-postcard perfect place to live. Who could imagine the controversy that was hidden just out of view?

Death of a Water District

3

Buying a Dam But Forgetting to Pay for It

Sugar Pine Dam was originally built by the Bureau of Reclamation in 1982. It was intended to be part of the grand Central Valley Project (CVP).

The CVP provides irrigation and municipal water to much of California's Central Valley. It regulates and stores water in reservoirs in the water-rich northern half of the state and transports it down the water-poor San Joaquin Valley.

It allowed major cities to grow along rivers in the San Joaquin Valley which previously would flood each spring. This transformed the semi-arid desert environment into productive farmland.

The Sugar Pine Dam was created to support the massive Auburn Dam to be built on the North Fork of the American River east of the town of Auburn, California.

When a seismic fault was discovered beneath the dam site, construction was halted. Plans for building the Auburn Dam were abandoned.

When it became clear that the Auburn Dam Project was not going forward, the Sugar Pine Dam and treatment plant became surplus inventory.

Although it cost $71 million to build, the Bureau of Reclamation offered to sell the dam lock, stock, and spillway for a mere $3 million.

It was an offer too good to pass up.

The PUD was able to secure a bond from the Bank of New York and the transaction was completed.

That's when things at the district started to go wrong.

4

False Economies

Like most public water districts in California, the Foresthill PUD is controlled by a board of five publicly elected residents from the community. No experience is required to be on the water board. No qualifications are needed. As long as a person receives a majority of votes in the election, they have a job on the board.

As happens in many water districts, some board candidates run unopposed. Simply placing one's name on the ballot assures a position on the board.

While this meets the legal requirements for a publicly elected board, it does not assure that sound management decisions get made.

Historically, the Foresthill PUD board and management had used a strategy of "deferred maintenance" to keep water rates artificially low.

"Deferred maintenance" is a polite term for not repairing or replacing the system as it ages. It shoves the economic burden of maintaining a water delivery system into a hazy and distant future.

A second strategy was to ignore a simple economic fact: During a period when costs for everything from medical insurance to gasoline were skyrocketing, the cost of running the district was also escalating.

During the period from 2003 to 2011 inflation rose 23%. A gallon of gasoline went from $1.95 to $2.94.

During this same period, the district's rates stayed flat at $22.00 per month.

With the added cost of paying for $3 million in bonds the board and management made a very interesting decision about their water rates.

They left them alone.

It's not uncommon for publicly elected officials to have their decisions swayed by concerns over their popularity. This leads to decisions that relieve their stress levels short-term, but create much bigger problems long-term.

The analysis showed that it would cost about $12 per ratepayer per month to fully meet the bond obligation and pay for the dam.

After some discussion, the board decided that they were only comfortable adding a $6.50 per month fee to pay the bond. So, that was where the fee was set.

Since the first year's payment on the bond included a pre-paid interest payment, the numbers worked for the first year. After that, there was no plan for how to meet the required bond repayment.

This set a series of events into motion. As you might suspect, things were soon to get much worse.

Death of a Water District

5

Raising Rates: A Decade of Increases All at Once

Financial reports are some of the most misunderstood management tools available. For some people they are as mysterious as ancient hieroglyphs on a pyramid wall. For others, they are a clear picture of the state of an organization's financial health.

At the Foresthill PUD it's hard to say if management was or wasn't sharing financial information over the previous decade, or if the board just didn't want to see the writing on the wall. The message in those reports was incredibly clear.

The district was in financial trouble. Deep trouble.

Every year the district received audited financial reports from outside accountants. They showed that in 2003

—the year the district bought the Sugar Pine Dam—the district was already losing money.

Because of the way the bond that purchased the dam was structured, a small pool of reserves was created. This financial cushion standardly allows a district to have a transition period as a new rate structure is put in place.

This bond cushion helped the bottom-line number at Foresthill to be positive for the next two years.

But it didn't change the fact that the cost of running the district was actually greater than the funds being collected. The pool of reserves created by the bond was consumed.

By 2006, the district was again experiencing heavy losses. *Those losses continued unabated for the next five years.*

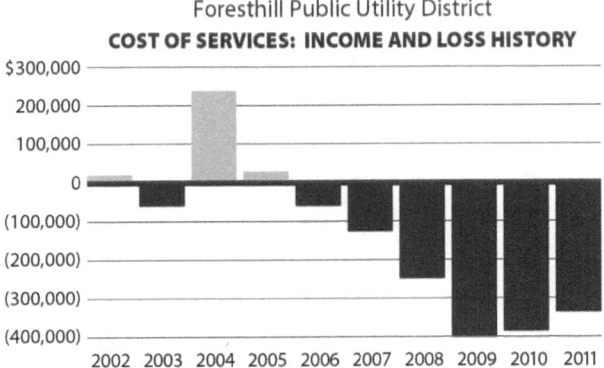

Reserve funds were sucked dry just to operate. The district stopped anything other than the most critical repairs on the water system.

One of the key mandates from the California Department of Public Health is that any water district in the state must be able to sustain itself.

That was not happening in Foresthill.

A look back at the water rates being charged shows that rates were kept constant from 1993 to 2001. During this same period, inflation was increasing steadily.

Expenses were rising, but rates were kept constant. The district was losing ground every year.

There was an increase of $3.00 per month in 2006, followed by a second increase of $2.50 per month in 2008. They were nowhere near enough to offset the mounting losses.

The district was still hemorrhaging vast amounts of money.

In 2010 the situation was critical enough that the district finally decided to take action. They instituted a dramatic rate increase, nearly doubling monthly rates from $27.50 to $48.21 per month.

This increases hit ratepayers like a

two-by-four to the back of the head. They were stunned and outraged.

The increase was enacted without any program that clearly explained to ratepayers why the increase was needed. A sense of betrayal and distrust spread throughout the community almost overnight.

Ironically, the increase was still not enough to actually solve the financial situation.

A storm was brewing. And it was going to be a monster.

6

Measure B Rears its Ugly Head

There was an out-of-town developer who for more than a decade had been talking about building a major housing project in the Foresthill area. While this had been discussed and many people in the community hoped it would bring jobs to the area, nothing materialized.

Of course, fundamental for any major housing development is access to water.

A typical process is that a developer submits plans for review, estimates the water requirements for the development, and requests to connect to the local water system. This results in a review of the plan, and if everything is correct it is approved to move forward.

That didn't happen in Foresthill.

No plan for the future development was submitted for review. Instead, the developer tried to use the county to take water rights away from the Foresthill PUD. Later there was an unsuccessful lawsuit against the district to attempt to take over water rights.

The PUD's legal team was kept busy defending the district. The money spent on legal fees could have paid for a four-year education at Stanford University.

Some people theorized that a scheme had been hatched to force the PUD into insolvency so the developer could take over the district. That would provide the needed control over water rights to bypass the usual channels.

With the sudden jump in water rates and a failure to build any support in the community, many people were already unhappy with the PUD.

The district's board then made another critical error.

Within weeks of the rate increase, they approved a 10% increase in the employee benefits package.

For a small community facing economic hardship, this was gasoline added to the fire.

At the time, three of the five seats on the water district board were up for reelection. With the election just a few months away, the composition of the board was about to change.

Even more important, with a majority of votes on the board becoming available, control of the district was up for grabs.

A group of disgruntled ratepayers were selected and funded to run in the November election. Several credible reports indicated that the primary source of funding for the three candidates came from the out-of-town developer.

As you might predict, these hand-picked candidates all won.

The sudden shift of power was not lost on the long-time general manager. For a few decades he had been able to run things as he wished. A look at the records shows that repairs and replacement of the system were virtually ignored. Reporting requirements for the bonds had been reported inaccurately. Transparency was lacking in all areas of operations and finances.

Facing a bleak and increasingly hostile future, the general manager found it convenient to retire.

Unbelievably, an even bigger problem then presented itself.

In reaction to the massive and unexplained rate increase and the employee benefit boost, a measure was placed on the ballot that mandated the water district roll its rates back to levels charged in 2008. The measure's passage would remove the district's ability to set rates based on the cost of service. Even worse, those rates would be locked in by law.

Remember that the district was hemorrhaging red ink in 2008. A few years later, with everything costing more, this measure guaranteed that the district would collapse.

It was known as Measure B. With existing negative sentiment and well-funded supporters promoting its passage, it quickly gained popularity.

Wild claims of financial waste at the PUD were being disseminated. The facts that the district was not covering its true cost of operation were unknown or ignored.

Residents were already frustrated about the overall negative economy and financial problems at the state and national level. Turning locally, the district became the focus of their anger.

The district then made yet another critical error.

They did nothing.

There was no information program to educate the community. There was no attempt to counter the misinformation that was running rampant. There were no meetings within the community with open and frank discussions.

When the election came, it was a rout. Measure B won by a vote of 63% Yes to 37% No.

The demise of the Foresthill Public Utility District was all but assured.

Death of a Water District

7

With a Gun to their Heads, the Board Wakes Up

There are a number of theories about what happened next.

Some theorize that the pressure of responsibility and mounting legal challenges was too great.

Some think that despite dramatically cutting staff, there was a realization that the district still couldn't operate under the mandated restraints.

Others think that a streak of conscience forced some board members to have second thoughts.

While the stated reasons varied, the result was indisputable. The newly elected board members started to resign.

With each vacancy, a new person

was appointed. These replacement board members, however, arrived with a different attitude. Rather than wanting to tear the district down, they had a desire to turn the district around.

After only five months on the job, the replacement general manager resigned. He was replaced by an interim general manager to keep things operating until a new general manager could be found.

The situation was grim.

The district was now down to six employees and was operating below health and safety requirements.

The system was breaking down and there were no funds to replace anything.

A series of unresolved legal actions would further drain funds.

The district was operating at a loss. The rates were locked in by Measure B.

And, around town the water district was as popular as a carnivore at a vegetarian conference.

One thing was clear. It was time for a change in Foresthill.

8

A Stranger Comes to Town

The Foresthill Bridge over the North Fork of the American River is the highest bridge in California. It's also the 4th highest bridge in the United States.

Originally constructed to accompany the unbuilt Auburn Dam, the bridge stands 731 feet above the riverbed.

It is the lifeline that connects Foresthill to the rest of the world.

The sky was crystal clear as Leo Havener steered his vehicle across the bridge for his first day as the new general manager of the Foresthill PUD.

Leo has a history of taking troubled districts and turning them around. As he negotiated the twists and turns of the mountainous Foresthill Road, he knew there was a big challenge ahead.

In most cases, the committee who hires a general manager will give an overview of the situation. They detail the positives and touch on the negatives. The catch is that they almost always leave something out.

In his gut and from past experience, Leo knew this. The board of the PUD hadn't painted a rosy picture. In fact, they actually stated that the situation was dire. The question was: just how bad could it be?

He was about to find out.

9

So What Was Really Going On?

An interim general manager had been hired to execute the layoffs and cuts necessitated by Measure B. Staffing levels had been cut to the bone.

Four water operators were left to operate a dam and a water treatment plant built using 1970s-era equipment with no automation. The operations crew had to keep 50 miles of aging pipeline functioning.

It was a disaster waiting to happen.

One person remained to handle all billing, administrative tasks, and customer service queries. By mid-morning each day, she was exhausted.

All financial functions were delegated to a part-time CPA who worked only one day a week.

And of course, there was the recently recruited general manager.

In the first conversation, the interim general manager looked at Leo with an expression of disgust. She said, "this never had to occur. It was all self-inflicted by the management and the board."

Leo continued his hunt for vital information about the district.

The annual operating budget just barely met the most technical definition of the term. It was three pages long and lacked any backup information for any of the numbers.

A quick review showed that despite the severe austerity program, the budget was operating at a $40,000 deficit for the year. Operating reserves had been depleted to a scant $7,500.

One long-time board member revealed that their master strategy was "to make cuts, then go through the year and see what to do next."

More bad news was about to appear.

In reviewing the district's audits of previous years, Leo suspected that the bond requirements were not being met. He asked to see the bond document. No one could find it. A week of searching turned up nothing. Finally, it was found tucked in an unmarked binder at the bottom of a bookshelf.

A half hour later, Leo's worst fears were confirmed.

Most bond agreements include legally binding requirements called a bond covenant. In this case, the requirement was that operating revenues must exceed operating expenses by 25% (1.25 times).

In running the numbers, Leo realized that the district had not met its covenant for a number of years. This meant that the Bank of New York could pull its bond at any time.

Since the collateral for the bond was the dam, the bank could effectively foreclose on the district and become the owner of the dam whenever they chose.

Even worse were the required written confirmations that the bond requirements were being met. Each was signed by the recently retired general manager.

They were lies.

This not only meant the district could be lost, it meant that they were potentially facing Federal Securities and Exchange Commission violations as well.

It was time to start taking action.

Death of a Water District

10

Recruiting Allies and a Strategy for Survival

Leo knew that it was going to take a team of people to remedy the situation.

He was impressed with the legal team. They had a good grasp of the situation and were providing sound legal strategies. The law firm had been around since 1959 and they focused on water and water-related resource law.

What was missing was someone to develop and coordinate the community relations element.

The district had been out of touch with its ratepayers for decades. The rate increase which had been shoved down the community's throat, followed by the large increase in the staff's benefits package had left the community with bitter feelings towards the PUD.

So now – with its credibility at an all time low – the district's challenge was to turn a community of critics into district supporters.

It was time to make a phone call.

Richard Wilson is well-versed in crises communications. He has a history of taking complex situations and distilling them to their simple essence so they make sense to an average person on the street.

Leo and Richard had worked together before. They were no strangers to distressed water districts where a major turnaround was needed.

A few years earlier, they had worked with a water district where a 48% rate increase was required. It was not met with enthusiasm by the public.

At the original public hearing the hall was filled with angry ratepayers who spilled out into the hallway. The story of that meeting ended up on the front page of the local paper.

A few months after the rate-increase communications program had been implemented, the final rate increase meeting was a non-event. The meeting hall was all but empty.

Four ratepayers showed up to speak. Three were resigned to the necessity of the increase, but still didn't like the idea. The fourth spoke out in favor of the increase.

The entire rate hearing process took only twenty minutes.

Leo knew what to do. The call was made. Richard arrived in Foresthill the following day. After evaluating the situation and meeting with the key players, a proposal was put before the board. They gave their approval.

Then an unusual and shocking public relations approach was developed.

The district was going to tell the truth.

Death of a Water District

11

An Unorthodox Plan

It's against human nature to openly discuss failures and shortcomings. It may be false pride or fear of ridicule that makes our first thought to hide whatever is wrong.

That's why the PUD board was skeptical when the plan was presented. The plan was actually quite simple. Perhaps that's what made it so effective.

The first step of the proposed plan was to let the community know that the district was insolvent and on the verge of closing. Rather than trying to make excuses or deny the facts, the plan was to acknowledge that there had been some big mistakes in the past.

It meant showing the financial condition of the district in clear, direct terms. The truth was not pretty, but it was a pivotal part of the communications strategy: changing the topic of discussion.

Critics of the district had been claiming that it was not well run. They claimed that there were massive amounts of waste and frivolous spending. It was a message that made its point and got Measure B passed.

By openly showing the dire condition of the district and acknowledging that there were errors in the past, the conversation could shift. It could move on and deal with the looming disaster.

The issue would be transformed to, "Do you want to give up your water district?"

With that, bashing the district would become unimportant. The new message focused on the inevitable result if things were allowed to continue as they were.

What would happen if the district failed? What would be the real impact on the community?

A first public meeting was scheduled. It was held at the largest meeting room in the area, the Foresthill Veterans Memorial Hall. It's a large meeting room used for everything from weddings to special events.

When word got out that the water district was on the verge of failure, the public came in droves. Each of the room's

175 of chairs quickly filled. More chairs were found. Those filled too. Finally, the late arrivals stood jammed together in the back of the hall.

A presentation was given which explained the situation in clear, direct terms. Within the audience, there was general shock and disbelief.

Most people hadn't thought much about their water district. Since the district had not been informing the public about their situation, it was disturbing to suddenly learn what was actually happening.

The Certified Public Accountant who had audited the financials verified that the district was indeed operating at a loss.

A graph showed that the district had been losing money for years. The reserves were effectively gone.

It was explained that the State of California would not allow the water district to stop functioning. The likely process would be that another private company would be brought in to operate the district.

That would mean that the 50 miles of pipelines, the treatment plant, the dam, and all the water behind it would be turned over to someone else.

A new reality was beginning to sink in.

As the next step in the process, Leo announced the formation of a Citizen's Advisory Committee. This group would review the situation, get answers to questions, and make recommendations.

It was the start of a brand new way of operating.

12

Building Trust

The Citizen's Advisory Committee included 25 members from the community. They ranged from business people who worked in the State's Capital to a feisty 85-year-old grandmother and her daughter.

Four meetings were scheduled. The first meeting provided a complete overview of the state of the district. It included financial reports and photos of the many leaks and failing pipes.

The financial projections showed that by June, the district would be completely out of money and would be forced to close.

While the information was understood, it was not what people wanted to hear. Not surprising, there was still a general feeling of distrust towards both the district and the "outsiders" who were running the meeting.

Next, tours were arranged to see the dam, antiquated treatment plant, the rusted water tanks, and the failing pipelines that had been recently pulled from the ground.

The committee was starting to get a clearer understanding of the true state of the district.

The next meeting focused on possible scenarios. One was that the district closed, the State of California would step in and give the district and its assets to one of the large private water companies.

Another scenario was that the community would keep the district, resulting in an unavoidable rate increase to cover the true cost of operation.

Important in this scenario was the resulting rate increase. Although it would be substantial, it would be less than the increases which would be put in place by a new, private water company.

More important, it would keep the district a public utility, controlled by the community. And it would keep the ample water supply under local control.

The committee was asked to come back with their recommendations. At the final meeting a consensus was reached.

The Community Advisory Committee clearly stated that the control of the district should be kept local.

The strategy of telling the truth and getting the community involved in the process was paying off.

But the problems were far from over.

Death of a Water District

13

The Opposition Strikes Back

There was a subversive in the Citizens Advisory Committee.

John (not his actual name) had always been a contentious member of the committee. He would argue with any information provided, all the way down to the actual type of pipe in the ground.

It was clear from early on that he wasn't interested in developing solutions. He just wanted to focus on problems.

He claimed that the audited financials were lies. He claimed the information about the number of people needed to safely operate the district was falsified. Despite photos to the contrary, he claimed the need to begin replacing leaking pipes was all a scam.

To say he was not a positive contributor to the process would be an epic understatement.

Then the weekly newspaper hit the newsstands. In it was a letter to the editor written by John claiming that the Citizen's Advisory Committee's recommendations were all a sham.

What was not lost on the rest of the committee was the submission date. In order for the letter to have been included when the newspaper was published, it had to have been written before the committee sorted out its final recommendations.

John had one goal — to discredit anything and everything that the district was doing.

At that point John also became the front man for the opposition's stand against the water district.

People have speculated as to why he took up this fight. The most suspicious members of the community pointed out the he was an out-of-work contractor. His actions were aligned with the desires of the out-of-town developer.

Some believe that the promise of substantial future work was the motivation. Some believe that money changed hands.

Whatever the case, a torrent of negative, inflammatory letters to the editor started hitting the paper. This was the same strategy used to successfully sell Measure B to the public. It was back in full force.

There were now two factions in the community. One was saying that the district should be saved. The other was saying that it was all a pack of lies devised for the PUD to continue ripping off the community.

Caught in the middle was the bulk of the community. They were confused and wondered which side was right?

Death of a Water District

14

A Bold Gamble: Creating Measure C

Even with the support of the Citizens Advisory Committee, there was a major obstacle to overcome.

Passing Measure B had locked the water rates into a non-viable range. It didn't matter what the board of directors or district management wanted to do. Those water rates were now the law. And the law assured that the district would go bankrupt and stay that way.

There was only one solution that had any chance of success: Get Measure B repealed by the voters.

It would not be an easy task to accomplish. Measure B had been passed by a 63% majority of the public just 12 months before.

The challenge would be to get the majority of the public to change their minds despite the ongoing misinformation campaign. And finally, those people had to be motivated enough to get out and vote.

There was no other option. If Measure B stayed in place the water district would be dead. A glance at the financial reports showed that time was running out.

A draft of a proposed measure was created to repeal Measure B. The district's legal counsel crafted it carefully so that it was simple, direct, and easy to understand.

The board of directors approved the measure and it was submitted to the Placer County Election Office to be put on the ballot. Fittingly, the measure to repeal Measure B was named Measure C.

It would be up for a public vote just 12 weeks later.

Naturally, there was just one more problem. As a public utility the water district could not fund any campaign activity that encouraged people to vote one way or another. Public funds cannot be used to influence an election.

The district could, however, provide information about the state of the district and the probable effects of its collapse.

The district had to stick to the facts. At the same time, it had to be very careful to never tell people how they should vote.

An independent group of citizens formed the "Yes on Measure C" committee. At the same time the "No on Measure C" committee quickly got organized.

In the middle, the district's public information campaign of "What happens if the water district fails and a new company takes over" was drawn up.

The battle lines were drawn. All parties were ready to engage. There was only going to be one shot at success. Failure was not an option.

Death of a Water District

15

A Lucky Break

As with any measure that is put on the ballot in California, written arguments both for and against are prepared. Both are included in an information pamphlet sent to every voter.

None of the arguments can be more than 300 words long. Written arguments are a powerful tool since many voters use them to decide how they'll actually vote.

A good written argument needs to be clear, concise, and not use a lot of technical jargon. If voters start to get confused, their trust level drops. Without a degree of trust, people will not vote your way.

Richard carefully crafted the written argument. It was then sent to the legal team to make sure that it fully complied with all rules and regulations. Then, it went back to Richard to assure that the legalese added by the lawyers was translated into plain, everyday language.

Here is the exact text from the voter pamphlet:

Arguments For Measure C

Measure C repeals and corrects the mistakes made by Measure B that are putting the survival of your water district at risk.

Measure B forced water rates back to their level in 2008. The problem is that when Measure B was written, no one bothered to see if the 2008 rates were viable. They weren't. Those rates are even less workable in 2012 when everything from food to gasoline costs more.

Measure B assured that the district could never cover its operating costs. That is exactly what is happening. Audited financials show that the district lost money for the past 6 years in a row.

Despite massive cutbacks and deferring maintenance that pushed the system to the edge of failure, the district is still on the verge of closing its doors.

What happens if the water district is forced to close? Placer County and the State of California will step in and turn over the operation to a company with deep pockets, and a track record of running water districts.

The downside is that this new company can also set water rates with Foresthill residents having virtually no say in the matter. Historically, this means the rates will go up much higher than if the district was locally operated.

Also, the new organization would control the water rights for our water supply.

Effectively, you will lose control over your water supply and be forced to pay much higher rates.

Undo the mistakes of Measure B by voting Yes on Measure C.

Measure C keeps control of the local water rights in the hands of Foresthill residents.

Measure C keeps an outside company from setting your water rates without your input.

Measure C saves your water district.

The proper forms were hand delivered to the election office the day before they were due.

The deadline for filing came and went. Surprisingly, no arguments against Measure C were submitted.

It was a lucky break. The "No on C" opposition group had not been careful about watching their deadlines.

That meant that the voter information pamphlet would now only include the argument for "Yes on C." There would be no opposition.

It gave a distinct advantage to the "Yes on C" supporters. The question on everyone's mind was, would it be enough?

16

The Battle of Foresthill

Newspapers in small communities are read differently than they are in big cities. In small communities, the weekly paper is reviewed with a careful attention to detail. A letter to the editor in a local paper is often read as often as the front page headline news.

That's where the battle began. Letters to the editor started to appear. The "No on C" group took an early lead. Many people believe that all utilities or governmental groups are over-funded, wasteful, and needlessly bureaucratic. Not surprising, those were the themes of the letter campaign and they resonated with large numbers of people.

Meanwhile, the "Yes on C" forces began a campaign of door-to-door canvasing and road signs. The message of "Save our Water" was one that people understood and found important.

The water district began a series of informational videos that were shown via their website.

They were inexpensively produced videos and they looked it. Because the public concern was that the district was wastefully overspending, these were budget productions.

Nevertheless they put across the facts that people needed to know to make an informed decision.

They explained the past mistakes of not properly funding the water district. They showed the deteriorating pipelines and problematic under staffing. They reviewed the dire financial situation that would result in the district's collapse by June if things were not changed.

Most important, they talked about the Sugar Pine Dam and the loss of this vital resource if the district failed. They made the point that much of the interest private water companies had in taking over the district was to control the water behind the dam.

If local ownership and control of the water was lost, Foresthill would have much less control over its own destiny.

As election day drew nearer, tensions rose. During the night one side's signs would occasionally be vandalized only to be steadfastly repaired the following day. There was a lot of scowling on the street.

The only people who seemed to be enjoying the situation worked at the local newspaper. With all of the controversy, papers were getting snapped up off the newsstands. Everyone wanted to know what the other side had said.

With election-based ads being placed, advertising revenue for the paper rose dramatically as well.

As a small community there were no professional polling services that focused on the election in Foresthill. There were no projected results on television or radio. The consensus at the local barbershop was that election was too close to call.

The following day would decide if the Foresthill Public Utility District would be closing its doors for good in only twenty-five days.

Death of a Water District

17

The Smoke Clears, Who's Won?

From the June 8, 2012 edition of the Mountain Democrat Newspaper that provided election results:

Foresthill PUD Measure C overturns Measure B

The saga of Foresthill Public Utility District reached another breathtaking moment. On the precipice of extinction as a public utilities district, Foresthill was saved by a positive vote in the primary election on June 5. General Manager Leo Havener had stated loud and clear that if the district-sponsored Measure C did not pass, Foresthill PUD would close its doors at the

> *end of June. The measure did pass, but the district isn't out of danger yet.*

The measure passed with 69.38% of the voters saying yes.

It's interesting that this occurred even though the voters knew that the next step would be to have a dramatic rate increase. While no one liked that scenario, it was clearly better than experiencing even higher rates and losing control over the water supply.

This was a historic moment, since no other water district in the state had ever faced a similar challenge. The district had prevailed.

All that was needed was for the board to implement a rate study to determine proper, viable rates, and begin the standard public process for implementing new water rates.

A program had been created that outlined exactly what to do. It detailed what would be needed to restore the district operationally and financially. The board simply needed to approve the plan so it could move forward.

Instead, the board had a different idea.
They fired the general manager.

They fired the consultant.

They dropped the plan to complete the turnaround.

Despite the dramatic change in public opinion, despite the success of the election, despite a clear plan to move forward, they simply pulled the plug.

Death of a Water District

18

What?

No one outside of the five board members of the Foresthill Public Utility District really knows what caused the sudden reversal.

The board had hired a new general manager to come in, turn things around, and save the district.

They brought in a ratepayer relations expert to facilitate communications with the public and fix public sentiment.

As a result, the public learned that deferring repair and replacement of the disintegrating pipes and treatment plant had put the community at risk.

They now knew that staffing levels were below what was considered "safe" by the California Department of Public Health. The staffing needed to be returned to proper levels or they would face being shut down by the State.

Measure C was an overwhelming success. It earned the highest margin of victory for any item on the ballot during that election.

It was well known that voting "Yes on Measure C" would also mean an increase in their water rates so the district could begin to operate viably. The public had given a clear mandate that they wanted to save the district.

Yet unbelievably the board decided not to follow through on the plan that would make the district viable.

Since their discussions occurred behind closed doors, there is no public record as to why they made their decision.

But the fact remains that what they did do was stop.

It would be another full two years before the district would finally decide to follow the advice provided by their turnaround team.

They developed a five-year rate structure with known rate increases for each of the five years. Whether these will provide the necessary funds to restore the district is still unknown.

The most important legacy of the Foresthill Public Utility District and the battle for its survival are the lessons that it provides to the leadership of other similar organizations.

Those five key lessons are detailed in the following chapters.

Death of a Water District

19

Lesson One: Whiskey is for Drinking; Water is for Fighting Over

It turns desert into productive land. It's critical for communities to exist and grow. It's vital for survival.

It's no wonder that people can get passionate about the subject.

Part of the emotion comes from the public feeling completely at the mercy of the water district. Effectively, the ratepayer has no choice. They need water to survive. They have no competing water source they can turn to. So, no matter their desires, they have to pay whatever increase is decided, whenever it's decided.

The emotions generated have little

to do with the actual dollars or decisions involved. The reaction comes from the lack of control.

But when it comes to water, things are not always as they appear.

In Foresthill, a developer had recruited and funded three candidates for the water district's governing board. When they all won, the developer had effective control over the utility.

Ultimately, it was the board's actions that fueled the public backlash that became Measure B.

Everyone who comes to a public meeting, runs for office, or writes a letter to the editor has an agenda. Sometimes their agenda is openly disclosed. Sometimes it is hidden. Sometimes that agenda is altruistic. Sometimes it is self-serving.

It is one of the reasons why people's actions regarding a water issue may not make sense. Unless you know the person's real agenda, it can be difficult to understand their actions.

The one thing that you can be certain of is that most reactions will be passionate.

Water amplifies people's responses. While a rate increase of $3 a month is less than an espresso drink at Starbucks, it has the potential to raise people's fury.

Take the time to understand not just what your ratepayers think about the district, *but why they think it*. Then you can address their real concerns.

Don't be surprised if you bump into opposing viewpoints. Some people are pro-growth. Others are anti-growth. There is probably no decision that would make all groups happy.

It is the nature of public utilities. It is the nature of water.

Death of a Water District

20

Lesson Two: Unreal Rates are a Ticking Time Bomb

The roots of the problems at Foresthill began two decades before Measure B was proposed. Sadly, the district's own general manager and board created them.

The management principal is simple. In an environment where costs of operation are constantly rising, any district needs to increase rates just to hold its own.

It's the nature of a public utility. A typical business can increase its revenue by adding more customers or adding new services.

By definition, a water district has 100% of the customers within its boundaries. So there's little opportunity to add new customers within the boundaries of the service area.

It's also very difficult to expand into other services to offer the public. You are limited by the constraints of being a utility.

As a result, the only way to increase revenue is to raise rates.

Since rates need to cover the true cost of service, when operation costs are rising, the fees collected also need to rise. If not, the entire utility is put at risk.

From the experience of being involved in a number of rate increases at a number of different districts, one thing has become clear. Ratepayers would rather have a series of small incremental increases than a single, large, shocking one.

Had the Foresthill board simply raised their rates slightly each year (2003-2011), they would never have gone into a deficit position.

All that was needed was a series of small annual increases that translated to $1.60 a month.

While no ratepayer likes any increase in rates, $1.60 a month is barely perceptible. If the increase is gradual, the shock and dismay that results from a dramatic hike can be avoided.

Had that simple strategy been used, the Foresthill drama never would have happened. There would have been money to repair and replace the infrastructure. Staff levels would have been maintained.

The Foresthill PUD would have been a properly funded, smooth-running operation. Instead, it became the poster-child for mismanagement.

Holding rates flat when costs are rising is simple, long-term mismanagement. The pressure builds until, finally, the situation explodes into a public relations disaster.

In Foresthill, this lack of foresight nearly killed the district.

Death of a Water District

21

Lesson Three: Treat Your District Like a Car

The ideal way to operate any type of facility is to care for it on an ongoing basis and to plan on replacing infrastructure as it wears out.

An example of this strategy done well is the Golden Gate Bridge. It is continuously repainted to protect it from the highly corrosive salt air.

There is also an ongoing project to replace rivets that have rusted. These steps help assure that the bridge stays in operation and has the longest life possible.

In running any district, two of the most obscene words you can use are "deferred maintenance."

What that term really means is that

the district is not planning for future operations. The current board is pushing today's problems onto a future board.

Imagine if you took that strategy with your car. You never changed the oil. You never replaced the tires. You never replaced the brake pads.

Short term, everything would be okay. In fact, you might even congratulate yourself for saving money on expensive car maintenance.

But we all know that it is simply a matter of time before something wears out or fails. Not only could this mean a potentially life-threatening accident, that failure is almost always much more expensive to repair.

It is much more costly to replace a blown engine than to have the oil changed every once in a while.

Pipes wear out. Treatment plants wear out. Well pumps wear out. It's not a matter of "if" it will happen, it's matter of "when" it will happen.

A portion of a district's annual operating budget needs to be dedicated to maintenance and replacement of aging infrastructure.

The phrase, "We're going to defer the

maintenance on the district" is code for: "I am irresponsible and am willing to gamble that someone else will solve this problem in the future."

While that may seem harsh, it's true.

Treat your district like a car that you want to last for a long time.

Your district will operate much more smoothly.

There will be fewer crisis repairs.

You'll save money.

You'll be serving the best interests of your ratepayers.

Death of a Water District

22

Lesson Four: Can Uninformed People Make Good Decisions?

There is something basic about human nature that the board and management of the Foresthill Public Utility District didn't include in their planning.

Most people cannot tolerate an information vacuum.

When people don't have the answer to a question, they feel compelled to answer the question with their best guess. Often, they will assume the worst.

It doesn't matter how unreal or untrue that answer may be. Once they decide on an answer, it becomes true for them.

That's what causes the spread of wild misinformation.

For decades, the district kept their ratepayers in the dark about true costs. They didn't disclose what it would take to pay for the dam and water supply they purchased. They didn't let anyone know that the deferred maintenance strategy was keeping the rates artificially low, while the system was deteriorating.

When they did finally execute a rate increase, they also made the mistake of dramatically raising the employee benefits packages. Without any explanation, the public concluded that the rate increase was mostly to overpay the staff.

When the public outcry began, the district made another mistake. They did nothing.

Wild claims started being made about the district around town. Without real information from the district, these claims became facts in the minds of the public.

So of course, when Measure B was proposed to force the rates to be rolled back, it found overwhelming support.

How did the district respond? Remarkably, they compounded their mistake. They still did nothing.

There was no information provided about the true cost of operation.

There was no information about the fact that rates had been kept falsely low by ignoring repairs and replacement of the pipes and infrastructure.

There was no information about the consequences of Measure B's passage.

So, the voters made what seemed to be the best choice possible. They passed Measure B.

That's why it took a carefully crafted and executed emergency communications program to make the correct information broadly known.

Most people are basically intelligent and well meaning. If they have the right information, they can make good choices. That is why a public information program is essential to running a successful district.

Death of a Water District

23

Lesson Five: The Time to Dig the Moat is Not When the Mongol Hoard is Cresting the Hill

A very common mistake is to wait until the last possible moment to begin communicating with ratepayers. One problem is that it gives a long period of time for misconceptions about the district to take hold. The other is that inevitably there is even more work to be done to correctly inform your public.

Starting sooner saves you work and ultimately saves you money.

In the case of the Foresthill PUD, they almost waited too long.

Fortunately, they were able to bring in an experienced turnaround general manager. Even then, the dire situation and the lack of resources almost made the turnaround impossible.

Knowing that the battle ahead was going to be fought in the minds of the public, the new general manager didn't hesitate to bring in the help needed for the ratepayer relations function.

So when do you want to increase your communications activity with your ratepayers? Today would not be too soon.

It takes a series of reminders for people to begin getting a message. (Ask any parent.)

Not everyone reads every piece of mail. Only a portion of your ratepayers read the paper. Even then, many people are selective readers, reading only parts of the paper, such as the sports section.

According to national averages, only about 1 in 10 people open bulk emails.

So there is no magic bullet. There is no single way to get a message out to 100% of your ratepayers. Even when you do reach your public, it often takes a number of reminders before a message takes hold and is understood.

The solution is to have an ongoing communications program that keeps your ratepayers informed.

Ideally, for something that can be as emotionally charged as a rate increase, you should start your program about 12 months before your first rate hearing.

Initially the program would begin by letting people know about the general needs of the district. Information about aging infrastructure starts to get the idea that things need to be replaced. Graphics that show the need for new sources of water help.

The more your ratepayers understand how you are being responsible in using their resources and how operating costs are increasing, the less likely they are to object to a rate increase.

The message is simple. Don't wait. Taking action quickly will yield better results with a higher degree of success.

Death of a Water District

24

The Next Step

The situation at the Foresthill Public Utility District can be a valuable example for other districts. It brings key management principles into sharp focus.

The lessons about these management principles illustrate better ways for your district to operate. By applying these lessons, you can avoid similar problems.

While those lessons may seem like simple common sense, it's not common for district boards and management to follow them.

Most wounds that districts suffer from are self-inflicted.

They needn't be.

This may mean that you need to operate quite differently than you have in the past. We are in challenging times.

Water is becoming ever more valuable. Infrastructure that has operated for decades is beginning to break down.

It's time for a change.

Assure that your board of directors and management team understand this information. Take these lessons and apply them. The result will be a more stable, secure, and successful district.

And that benefits every person in your community.

We wish you the best of success, a happy ratepayer base, and smooth operations in the future.

Regards,

Leo D. Havener and
Richard A. Wilson

Death of a Water District

About the Authors:

Leo D. Havener

Leo is an accomplished executive with over 35 years of experience working for special districts and public agencies. He is highly regarded as a general manager and consultant who straightens out challenged utilities.

In addition to his experience with public agencies, Leo had the unique opportunity to serve the citizens of Ceres, California, first as an elected City Council Member and then as their elected Mayor.

He has been a featured speaker for the American Water Works Association (AWWA), the Association of California Water Agencies (ACWA), and the California Special Districts Association (CSDA).

Leo's diverse educational background includes degrees in engineering and political science. In addition, he holds a Masters of Public Administration.

You can reach him at:
www.leohavener.com

Richard A. Wilson

Understanding, distilling, and effectively communicating ideas are skills at which Richard has excelled throughout his professional life. For him it is a lifelong passion. Over the past three decades, this fascination has driven him to successfully create programs for groups as diverse as technology companies to water districts.

Richard is a respected marketing veteran, author, and leadership expert. He has been a featured speaker at numerous business schools and national conferences including the American Water Works Association (AWWA).

He is the founder of Sentium Strategic Communications, a ratepayer relations firm grounded on practical, proven strategies to maximize effectiveness.

Based in Northern California, the Sentium team assists clients located throughout the United States.

You can get more information at: www.ratepayerrelations.com

Putting This Information to Work for You

If there are others you know who would benefit from these lessons, here are a few things you can do.

1. Get a copy of this book for all of your board members and management team.

2. Schedule a workshop for your board members and management team that will help you actively apply this information in your district.

3. Get direct consulting about managing your district or in implementing a ratepayer relations program.

   Get more information at:
   www.deathofawaterdistrict.com

www.ingramcontent.com/pod-product-compliance
Lightning Source LLC
Chambersburg PA
CBHW020925180526
45163CB00007B/2883